LIAM DAVIES

Covert Manipulation

Your Great Guide To Learn All About The World Of Manipulation, With The Techniques To Defend Yourself From Manipulation And Understand How It Works

Copyright © 2021 Liam Davies

All rights reserved.

© **Copyright 2021 - All rights reserved.**

The content contained within this book may not be reproduced, duplicated or transmitted without direct written permission from the author or the publisher.

Under no circumstances will any blame or legal responsibility be held against the publisher, or author, for any damages, reparation, or monetary loss due to the information contained within this book. Either directly or indirectly.

Legal Notice:

This book is copyright protected. This book is only for personal use. You cannot amend, distribute, sell, use, quote or paraphrase any part, or the content within this book, without the consent of the author or publisher.

Disclaimer Notice:

Please note the information contained within this document is for educational and entertainment purposes only. All effort has been executed to present accurate, up to date, and reliable, complete information. No warranties of any kind are declared or implied. Readers acknowledge that the author is not engaging in the rendering of legal, financial, medical or professional advice. The content within this book has been derived from various sources. Please consult a licensed professional before attempting any techniques outlined in this book.

By reading this document, the reader agrees that under no circumstances is the author responsible for any losses, direct or indirect, which are incurred as a result of the use of information contained within this document, including, but not limited to, — errors, omissions, or inaccuracies.

Table of Content

Introduction 4

Chapter 1. How To Defend Yourself From Manipulation Techniques 10

Chapter 2. Qualities of a Manipulative Person 16

Chapter 3. Victim of Manipulation 23

Chapter 4. Strategies for Seduction, a Person with Manipulation. 30

Chapter 5. Covert Emotional Manipulation 35

Chapter 6. Covert Manipulation in a Love Relationship 42

Chapter 7. How the Mind Works When It Is Manipulated? 48

Chapter 8. Hypnosis 54

Chapter 9. Office Politics or Sociopathic Tricks? – The Workplace Manipulators 60

Chapter 10. Human Behavior and Manipulation 66

Conclusion 72

Introduction

So far, I have briefly talked about a few manipulation techniques through personality traits and signs. However, it is important to be thorough about the techniques because there are dozens of techniques that manipulators use. Sometimes, they make up their techniques to gain control as they go through their job or relationship.

Foot in the Door Technique

The foot in the door technique is probably one of the most well-known forms of manipulation. Of course, the salespeople took the phrase a bit more literally than manipulators. While salespeople would place their foot in front of the door so the homeowner couldn't close it on them, manipulators take more of a mental and emotional stance towards this technique.

The first step manipulators use by asking for a small favor or "breaking the ice" through a small conversation. This helps the manipulators build a rapport with their target. For example, if they are trying to find a significant other, they will find a way to become compatible with their target. They will then ask the person questions about what they like and mention they enjoy the same things.

This technique is often how people get to know each other in a social setting. For example, have you ever been sitting at a club or coffee shop when someone came up to you and started small talk? They might have stated it was a busy night or a nice day. You might have agreed in some way, whether verbally or through your actions. Giving a reaction is letting the person keep their foot in the door. While you are probably just trying to be polite, they see it as a step into your life, depending on their motive.

Negative Reinforcement

Master manipulators will often use negative reinforcement to get you to stop doing something they don't like. This could be anything from going back to college or getting a job. Typically, they don't like anything that gives them a loss of control and threatens their environment.

When you start to do something they don't like, they will do something you don't like. This is the first step of negative reinforcement. They will continue to use negative reinforcement and other tactics to try to get you to stop doing what they don't like. Once they have manipulated you to stop, they will then stop.

Negative reinforcement works when the manipulator starts to do something you don't like because you won't do what they want you to do. To get the manipulator to stop doing what you don't like, you have to do what they request of you, even if you don't like it.

The main reason negative reinforcement is used is that it is more likely that you will do what they ask of you in the future without hesitation. This is especially true for manipulators who use any type of abuse to get you to stop doing something or to listen to them.

The Emotional Triangle

The emotional triangle is similar to a love triangle; however, it is used against you. The manipulator will use it to get you to do what they want. They will create a triangle with themselves, you, and a third person who is not directly involved in your relationship.

The manipulator will not hide the fact that they are interested in the third person, even if they aren't in truth. They will flirt with the person in front of you and even show affection toward the person. Sometimes they will use certain affections that you like, whether rubbing the person's back or hugging them.

While it might be obvious they like the other person. They will deny any type of affection in a confrontation. They will blame you, telling you that it is your insecurities and low self-esteem, which is making you believe this.

The emotional triangle's main goal is you become insecure about your relationship, which means you will work harder to make your significant other happy. You will do what they ask, even if you don't want to or feel uncomfortable taking on the assignment.

Establishing Similarities

The foot in the door technique can often lead manipulators into another technique where they establish similarities. For example, the manipulator might learn through observation or a friend who you like a certain coffee shop. Therefore, they will decide to run into you at the coffee shop, where they discuss how much you both enjoy the location and the coffee.

Manipulators will also mirror your actions. They will notice if you are putting your elbows on the table and do the same thing. They will notice your hand gestures and how often you smile. They will then mirror these actions as well. This is a psychological tactic that reaches into your subconscious mind. It makes you feel like you can trust the person because you feel more connected, even if you don't realize they mirror your actions and behaviors.

Fear-Relief Technique

Fear is a strong emotion and can often cause us to react in extreme ways. People are typically uncomfortable with fear, which means they will want to find a way to ease their fears. Because of this, manipulators commonly use the fear-relief technique as it allows them to gain the trust of their target by using emotion.

This technique is heavily used by manipulative people who create a fear in you to give you relief, which makes you more likely to listen to their requests time. You wait a couple of hours, and when they still don't return, you call their cell phone. They don't pick up. Another hour, you try calling them again but receive their voicemail. At this point, you start to become anxious about the situation. You have left dozens of text messages, and they don't answer their phone. You start to worry that something has happened to them. A couple of hours, they send you a text that says they are on their way home, and everything is fine.

When you confront your significant other as they walk in the door about what they were doing, they respond that you left, so they could too. They then tell you that as long as you do something like that to them, they can do it too.

Manipulators Will Put You on the Defense

Manipulators like to reach into your emotions because they are powerful. When you react with your emotions, you stop thinking, make irrational decisions, and have trouble remaining calm. This is how a manipulator wants you to react because conversations where you are calm and think rationally, are not in their favor.

Therefore, manipulators use a tactic where they will put you on the defense. This means that you will feel like you need to explain yourself. You have to defend how you feel, who you are, and what you believe. This is one of the strongest signs of manipulation, but people often don't notice it because it becomes common.

It is significant to understand that just because you find you are explaining something you believe to your significant other doesn't mean you are in a manipulative relationship. There are many times in a relationship that you might find yourself explaining why you support a cause your significant other doesn't or why you find something is fun when your partner doesn't. In a healthy relationship, you will find yourself explaining your beliefs and thoughts when your significant other wants to understand you to support you. You will also ask your loved ones to explain themselves so that you can treat them in the same way. In a manipulative relationship, your significant other will always put you on the defense, no matter what your action was. The only time you might not find yourself on the defense is if they approve of your behavior.

The Gaslighting Technique

Gaslighting is phrasing the manipulator will repeatedly use to make you believe a situation you remember is wrong. Some of the most common phrases include "You can't be serious," "I never said that," "You don't remember it correctly," "Are you crazy?" and "You imagine it." While you might feel that you are right, the manipulator will continue to stand by what they say, believe, or even give you their version of the situation. They might mix gaslighting with other tactics for you to start questioning yourself. They will continue to break you down through gaslighting or simply find a way to end the conversation.

Gaslighting is a very dangerous tactic because it is used to distort your reality. If used enough, you might start to feel that you are crazy or imagine all these situations. This will mentally and emotionally break you down even further, which will allow the manipulator to gain the upper hand as you start to distrust your thoughts, emotions, and abilities. You start to distrust your reality, making you believe that you do not see what you see, and you do not hear what you hear.

Traumatic One Trial Learning Technique

Manipulators are good at putting on an act. One technique that manipulators use to get you to listen to them better to keep you under control is traumatic one-trial learning.

When a manipulator uses this technique, they will become angry when they feel you have done something wrong. For example, if you come home later than you said you would, your significant other might yell, make you feel ashamed, or become verbally abusive. They will act in a way they know will make you fear their anger, so you are less likely to do something like that again.

Chapter 1. How To Defend Yourself From Manipulation Techniques

To avoid falling victim to manipulators, you have to build your defenses to prepare for any manipulative strategies they may try to use. The best way to build your defenses is by taking steps to improve your self-esteem and your willpower. However, as a point of caution, you should be very careful about building your defenses because you don't want to create restrictions that will keep you from living a fulfilled life.

For example, as you try to guard against manipulation, you can't act out of fear. You can't hide from the world just to avoid scenarios where someone might want to take advantage of you. Recall that the world is full of persons with dark personality traits who may harbor malicious intentions, so acting out of fear won't protect you from anyone. It will just make you more of a target. As you build your defenses, make sure that you start on the premise that you are willing to confront manipulators head-on, and you will never run away or recoil. If you act out of fear, you lose by default.

Acceptance

Acceptance is about assenting to the reality of a given situation. It's about recognizing that a certain condition or process is what it is, even if high levels of discomfort and negativity characterize it. It's about consciously submitting that something cannot be changed and that its reality is not subject to interpretation. It's about making peace with the situation that you are in. Acceptance is the opposite of denial. Denial can be a coping mechanism, one that can keep us from being overwhelmed by the reality of a given situation. However, denial does us more harm than good because unless we can accept something, we can't change it. We will be stuck looking for alternative interpretations and explanations for our prevailing circumstances.

Without acceptance, the door remains wide open for malicious people to exploit us. Take the example of a patient who is told that he/she is terminally ill. After seeking the opinions of several medical professionals and getting the same diagnosis, the patient is still left with the choice of either accepting or denying the situation. The one who accepts it will make peace and try to make the best of what little time he has. The one who stays in denial will become susceptible to tricksters who may offer "alternative cures," and he may end up losing all his savings paying such people so that in the end, he leaves his family with nothing. That is an extreme example, but it perfectly illustrates why acceptance is important in avoiding manipulation, even if the reality may seem too painful to accept.

The most crucial form of acceptance is self-acceptance. It refers to the state of being satisfied with yourself, the way you currently are. Self-acceptance is a kind of covenant that you make to validate, support, and appreciate who you are instead of constantly criticizing yourself and wishing you were someone else. Most people have trouble accepting themselves as they are. We are all in a constant strive for self-improvement. We want to be more successful, be wealthier, be more attractive, or be perceived more positively by others. Even the most accomplished among us have issues with self-acceptance.

In many ways, the desire to be a better version of yourself can be seen as a positive thing; it can help you study harder in school, work harder to earn a promotion at work or exercise more to get in shape. However, there is always room for improvement, so no matter how high you ascend, the dissatisfaction will always be there. It will make you vulnerable to manipulation by people who want to take advantage of your desires.

To defend against manipulation, you have to accept your reality, and you have to accept yourself. People tend to think that if they accept themselves, they won't try to improve—that couldn't be further from the truth. Accepting yourself means owning up to your flaws, and that gives you control over your life. With self-acceptance, attempts at self-improvement would come from within, so when you decide to change, you will.

Increase Awareness

Increasing your awareness means having a higher level of alertness when it comes to an understanding of what's going on in your environment. It means paying close attention to your surroundings and to the way people behave around you. The higher your level of awareness, the better you will be in adapting to your surroundings and understanding the motivations of the people you interact with.

When you become more aware, you will be able to catch on quickly when people try to manipulate you. Numerous of us tend to be preoccupied with our thoughts that we hardly ever notice the cues of the people we interact with. We tend to live life on autopilot, so when other people try to seize control over our lives, we only notice it when it's too late. If you increase your awareness, you will be equipped with the skills necessary to identify all the red flags, and you will be able to stop most manipulators in their tracks before they can do any real harm.

The first step towards increasing your awareness is to learn about the tendencies of manipulative people. Reading this puts you ahead of the curve; you now know enough to be able to spot people with ill motives, but you should understand that the worst kinds of manipulators are very good at concealing their motives, so you have to keep working on increasing your awareness.

To be truly aware of manipulative people, you have to approach all interactions with skepticism levels. We are not telling you to turn into a paranoid person who doesn't let anyone in; we are just saying that you should take a deeper look at each person you interact with. Try to study their body language and their words and see if they are trying to hide something.

Apart from increasing your awareness, you have to increase your self-awareness as well. Many people confuse those two things, but they entirely different concepts. Self-awareness is about understanding yourself. It's about having a clear concept of your personality. You have to examine yourself and figure out your strengths and weaknesses, values and motivations, and what kind of thoughts and emotions you are likely to have in specific situations. Self-awareness helps you understand both who you are and how other people perceive you.

Self-awareness works as a defense against manipulation because when you know who you truly are, it becomes more difficult for someone to alter your thoughts and perceptions. If you have strong and well-articulated values, it becomes harder for a manipulator to get you to abandon those values. People who like self-awareness are more likely to be gaslighted or subjected to other forms of mind control.

If you end up in a relationship with a manipulative person, self-awareness can help you keep your identity. Manipulators will try to tell you what to think and how to behave. Still, if you are self-aware, you will experience cognitive dissonance, and your brain will push back against any attempts at manipulation.

Detach with Love

Detaching with love is a defense against manipulation that is most commonly used by people who have loved ones who suffer from substance abuse problems. Even though it was conceptualized to help people deal with addicts, you can also work when dealing with manipulators.

Detaching with love is about showing love and compassion for others without taking responsibility for their actions. If the addict doesn't come home, you don't waste your time looking for them in the seedy parts of the city, you stay at home, and you do the things that benefit you and make you happy.

The point of detaching with love is to stop trying to control other people's lives, even if you are doing it for their good. The idea is that you accept that people are different from you and have their own free will.

Detaching from love can defend you from manipulation in many ways. Some manipulators want to exploit you by making you responsible for them. We have mentioned several times that some malicious people will take the submissive position in a relationship because they want your world to revolve around them. They want you to give them all your attention; that is how they control you. When you detach with love, you will learn to stop fixing everyone's problems. So, when the manipulator tries to play the victim to gain your sympathy, you will keep doing whatever is in your best interest, and you will tell him or her to take accountability for his or her actions.

Some manipulators may take up self-destructive habits because they want to dominate you by making you clean up after them. When they do this, you can detach with love by letting them follow the paths they have taken, no matter where they lead them. If they are causing you harm, you can get away from them, but leave your door open. If they find the right path in the future and regain control over their own lives, you can let them in again. You have to make it very clear that you will let them direct their own lives through your words and actions, and you won't take any responsibility for them.

Detaching with love is about accepting others for who they are and respecting them enough to let them be in charge of changing their own lives. When you feel responsible for someone, and he makes a choice that harms you both, you will frequently react with fear, anger, or anxiety. To detach with love, you have to learn to let go of those negative emotions.

Manipulators count on the fact that you will react in a predictable way to their machinations, but when you detach with love, you learn to calm yourself down and think about your role in the other person's life before you take any sort of action. This will keep you from falling into the traps that manipulators will set for you. Detaching with love builds your self-esteem because it allows you to put your own needs ahead of those trying to manipulate you.

Chapter 2. Qualities of a Manipulative Person

If you have ever heard the term "master manipulator," you might have an idea of a few manipulator personality traits. Most manipulators, especially people who are using it for their benefit, share similar characteristics. One factor to note is that there are easily noticeable traits and traits manipulators will hide well.

Manipulators Will Pressure You

A manipulator will pressure you into deciding before you are ready. They might start by doing this subtly at first and then increase their efforts. Their goal is to get you to cave as this will give them what they want.

Manipulators Are Experts at the Silent Treatment

If there is one main way to make a manipulator mad, it is not to give in. When a manipulator starts to feel threatened by your emotional and mental strength, they will resort to isolating you. For example, they might refuse to allow you to answer a question or completely ignore you.

Manipulators use this tactic to remain powerful. They want to make sure they assert their dominance.

Manipulators Will Bully You

Manipulators will do whatever they can to remain powerful, including bullying behavior. They will do whatever they can to shake your confidence as they want to make sure you don't feel emotionally and mentally stronger than them.

They will take part in this behavior anywhere; however, they often become more of a bully in public. This is because it allows them to embarrass you to the point you won't want to socialize with many people.

Manipulators Will Never Admit Their Faults

Manipulators will find someone else to blame, such as their parents, significant other, friends, and even children. They will also make up excuses when someone notices their weaknesses. For example, they might say that they didn't know certain information because someone never told them.

Manipulators Will Test Your Boundaries

No matter how strongly you discuss your boundaries with a manipulator, they will still test them. While they will act like they are sorry initially, telling you that they didn't realize this was a boundary, they don't feel this way. Testing your boundaries is a great way for a manipulator to learn what you will and will not put up with. They want to learn your breaking points to know what they can and cannot do right away. This doesn't mean that they won't cross your breaking points. They will just wait to do this until they have you within their webs.

Manipulators Don't Validate Your Feelings

Manipulators don't care about you as a person. They care about using you to get what they want. Therefore, they aren't going to spend time trying to make you feel better, ask you what is wrong, how your day went, or validate your feelings.

As humans, we need to have our emotions validated to work through them and maintain a healthy mindset. By not validating your emotions, manipulators can keep stronger control over you because you will start to lose your confidence, self-esteem, and self-image. You will become so overwhelmed with emotions; most of them negative, you will become depressed and stop caring about yourself. You might also stop talking to your friends and family. In general, you lose your interest in life.

This gives a manipulator the upper hand because you are more likely to do what they say. You will act how they want you to act. Even if you don't feel it is right, they will start to get you to believe that they are the only ones who care about you. Of course, this will further isolate you from anyone else you know and used to hang out with.

Manipulators Are Compulsive Liars

Manipulators are also known as compulsive liars. This is because they often distort facts to make them seem better than you or the best out of everyone. For a manipulator, it doesn't matter if the facts prove them wrong. They do not believe the facts.

However, their lying goes beyond facts. They will also use half-truths or withhold important information from you. This will allow them to maintain their leverage over you. For example, if you are working on a project with a manipulator, they will try to get information from their supervisor or project manager when you are not there. They will then inform you of what they were told but leave out a lot of information. They can then use this left-out information against you. They could lower your confidence in the project because you don't know everything your partner knows, or they could embarrass you in front of other people.

At this point in life, you have probably known about manipulative people. That is their mantra, many manipulative people have been practicing this art for a very long time, and as they say, practice makes perfect. Many people do not just immediately become manipulative. It can happen over time, generally, after the first time they have successfully gotten what they want, and they realize they can do it repeatedly. That is why it can be so difficult to tell when you are being manipulated because manipulators are not amateurs, so if you think you are being manipulated, remember it is not your fault. You have part of something that is much nuanced and complex, often making you feel as though you have done something wrong when that is not the case.

It would be so much easier if manipulative people signed on their backs, saying that they were indeed manipulators, but it's not that easy. They are usually very charming. One way to get you hooked is when true manipulation starts. They also adapt quickly to different situations very quickly, making it even more difficult to spot them. Unfortunately, this is all part of their game, making it even more complicated because they do change on a dime, and keeping you on your toes is what they are good at. Fortunately, they do typically stick to a certain script, if you will, that combines certain words and phrases, so that is one of the best and easiest ways to find out who in your life are the manipulators.

Traits of Manipulators

Playing the Victim

Many manipulators learn to play the victim, making it seem like they need help when they don't. They often do this by making you feel like you have caused a problem when this is not true. In reality, they are the ones that caused the issue, whatever it may be, and blame you because they do not want to take responsibility. This can be as simple as getting an apology from you or something bigger such as monetary gain. When you owed them nothing, to begin with, but they twisted it around so well, you feel as though you did do something wrong.

Hot and Cold

Manipulators can often be nice one minute and standoffish the next. This is hard to deal with because you don't know which person you will get when you see or talk to them. This is one of the easiest ways to prey on your fears and insecurities and keep you guessing. This is not a healthy friendship or relationship because the person being manipulated is constantly on their toes and worried about how they will treat them, always wondering if something they did to provoke this behavior. It might sound juvenile, but this can be very powerful in lowering someone's self-esteem, especially over a long time.

Aggressive

Many manipulators can take it passed being standoffish and can resort to being extremely aggressive or even vicious. They might not be physical, but they can wear another person down by using personal verbal attacks. All of this is done because that is how badly they want to get what they want. Often, they will not let up or stop until the other person is so worn down that they simply give in just to get the abuse to stop.

Lack of Insight

Many manipulative people lack insight when it comes to how to interact with others healthily. Instead, they truly believe that the only way to deal with situations is their way, and everyone else is wrong because their desires or needs are not being met. So, the scenarios and solutions they create will only benefit them at the expense of everyone else around them. This means that every friendship, relationship, and situation is about them, and everything else does not matter.

No Questions

Manipulative people do not question their behavior. They think they know what is right because it benefits them, which is the end of it. An average person knows how to read a situation and might understand, given certain circumstances, that their beliefs or opinion is wrong and can adjust it appropriately. A manipulative person does not do this. They just don't ask questions or wonder if the problem is them.

Lack of Boundaries

Part of being manipulative is putting their desire above everything else; part of this is not respecting other people's boundaries. They will crowd someone's spiritual, physical, emotional, and psychological space with absolutely no concern to them. This is often how they achieve their goals in the first place, by crossing these boundaries and exploiting the insecurities of others. A great way to think of this is to imagine them like a parasite, something that works in the natural world, but it is unacceptable for humans. Feeding off of someone else at their expense is weakening, demeaning, and exhausting.

Avoids Responsibility

One of the biggest traits of a manipulator is the inability to accept responsibility; everything is always someone else's fault. This does not mean that they do not know what responsibility is; on the contrary, they know what it is enough to blame someone else, just never themselves. Generally, they want you to take responsibility for their happiness, leaving you with no time or resources to get your own.

Preying on Sensibilities

Manipulators know that not everyone makes a great target, so they search out a certain type of person. They look for sensitive and conscientious people because they know this will increase their chances of trapping them into some sort of relationship. Finding the type of person who is kind, caring, feeling, and, most of all, the type of person who enjoys helping others is the perfect prey for them.

In the beginning, a manipulator will often cater to kindness and caring, usually praising the person for what a good person they are. Still, over time this will switch to praising them for what they can do for the manipulator. Again, this is not an overnight change, but one that takes time and is one reason it is so successful.

Disharmony

One common trait of a manipulator is to create disharmony amongst friend groups. They commonly talk negatively about everyone behind others' backs and enjoy stirring the pot. This keeps people uncomfortable, and they can do it in a way that makes them seem more trustworthy.

Chapter 3. Victim of Manipulation

Certain characteristics and behavioral traits make people more vulnerable to manipulation, and people with dark psychology traits know this full well. They tend to seek out victims who have those specific behavioral traits because they are essentially easy targets. Let's discuss 6 of the traits of the favorite victims of manipulators.

Emotional Insecurity and Fragility

Manipulators like to target victims who are emotionally insecure or emotionally fragile. Unfortunately, for these victims, such traits are very easy to identify even in total strangers, so it's easy for experienced manipulators to find them.

Emotionally insecure people tend to be very defensive when attacked or under pressure, making them easy to spot in social situations. Even after just a few interactions, a manipulator can gauge how insecure a person is with a certain degree of accuracy. They'll try to provoke their potential targets subtly and then wait to see how the targets react. If they are overly defensive, manipulators will take it as a sign of insecurity, and they will intensify their manipulative attacks.

Manipulators can also tell if a target is emotionally insecure if he/she redirects accusations or negative comments. They will find a way to put you on the spot, and if you try to throw it back at them or make excuses instead of confronting the situation head-on, the manipulator could conclude that you are insecure and, therefore, an easy target.

People who have social anxiety also tend to have emotional insecurity, and manipulators are aware of it. In social gatherings, they can easily spot individuals who have social anxiety, then target them for manipulation. "Pickup artists" can identify the girls who seem uneasy in social situations by the way they conduct themselves. Social anxiety is difficult to conceal, especially to manipulators who are experienced at preying on emotional vulnerability.

Emotional fragility is different from emotional insecurity. Emotionally insecure people tend to show it all the time, while emotionally fragile people appear to be normal, but they break down emotionally at the slightest provocation. Manipulators like targeting emotionally fragile people because it's very easy to elicit a reaction from them. Once a manipulator finds out that you are emotionally fragile, he will jump at the chance to manipulate you because he knows it would be fairly easy.

Emotional fragility can be temporary, so opportunistic manipulators often target people with these traits. A person may be emotionally stable most of the time. Still, he/she may experience emotional fragility when they are going through a breakup when they are grieving or dealing with an emotionally draining situation. The more sinister manipulators can earn your trust, bid their time, and wait for you to be emotionally fragile. Alternatively, they can use underhanded methods to induce emotional fragility in a person they are targeting.

Sensitive People

Highly sensitive people are those individuals who process information at a deeper level and are more aware of the subtleties in social dynamics. They have lots of positive attributes because they tend to be very considerate of others, and they watch their step to avoid causing people any harm, whether directly or indirectly. Such people tend to dislike any form of violence or cruelty, and they are easily upset by news reports about disastrous occurrences or even depictions of gory scenes in movies. Sensitive people also tend to get emotionally exhausted from taking in other people's feelings. When they walk into a room, they have the immediate ability to detect other people's moods because they are naturally skilled at identifying and interpreting other people's body language cues, facial expressions, and tonal variations.

Manipulators like to target sensitive people because they are easy to manipulate. If you are sensitive to certain things, manipulators can use them against you. They will feign certain emotions to draw sensitive people in so that they can exploit them.

Sensitive people also tend to scare easily. They have a heightened "startle reflex," which means that they are more likely to show clear signs of fear or nervousness in potentially threatening situations. For example, sensitive people are more likely to jump up when someone sneaks up on them, even before determining whether they are in any real danger. If you are a sensitive person, this trait can be very difficult to hide, and malicious individuals will be able to see it from a mile away.

Sensitive people also tend to be withdrawn. They are mostly introverts, and they like to keep to themselves because social stimulation can be emotionally draining for them. Manipulators looking to control others are more likely to target introverted people because that trait makes it easy to isolate potential victims.

Manipulators can also identify sensitive people by listening to how they talk. Sensitive people tend to be very proper; they never use vulgar language, and they tend to be very politically correct because they are trying to avoid offending anyone. They also tend to be polite, and they say please and thank you more often than others. Manipulators go after such people because they know that they are too polite to dismiss them right away; sensitive people will indulge anyone because they don't want to be rude, giving people maliciously away.

Emphatic People

Emphatic people are generally similar to highly sensitive people, except that they are more attuned to others' feelings and the world's energy around them. They tend to internalize other people's suffering to the point that it becomes their own. In fact, for some of them, it can be difficult to distinguish someone's discomfort from their own. Emphatic people make the best partners because they feel everything you feel. However, this makes them particularly easy to manipulate, which is why malicious people like to target them.

Malicious people can feign certain emotions and convey those emotions to emphatic people, who will feel them as though they were real. That opens them up for exploitation. Emphatic people are the favorite targets of psychopathic conmen because they feel so deeply for others. A conman can make up stories about financial difficulties and swindle lots of money from emphatic people.

The problem with being emphatic is that because you have such strong emotions, you easily dismiss your doubts about people because you would much rather offer help to a person who turns out to be a lair than deny help to a person who turns out to be telling the truth.

Emphatic people have a big-hearts, and they tend to be extremely generous, often to their detriment. They are highly charitable, and they feel guilty when others around them suffer, even if it's not their mistake, and they can't do anything about it. Malicious people have a very easy time taking such people on guilt trips. They are the kind of people who would willingly fork over their life savings to help their friends get out of debt, even if it means they would be ruined financially.

Malicious people like to get into relationships with emphatic people because they are easy to take advantage of. Emphatic people try to avoid getting into intimate relationships in the first place because they know that it's easy for them to get engulfed in such relationships and to lose their identities in the process. However, manipulators will doggedly pursue them because they know that they can guilt the emphatic person into doing anything they want once they get it.

Fear of Loneliness

Numerous people are afraid of being alone, but this fear is heightened in a small percentage. This kind of fear can be truly paralyzing for those who experience it, and it can open them up to exploitation by malicious people. For example, many people stay in dysfunctional relationships because they are afraid they will never find somebody else to love them if they break up with an abusive partner. Manipulators can identify this fear in a victim, and they'll often do everything they can to fuel it further to make sure that the person is crippled by it. People who are afraid of being alone can tolerate or even rationalize any kind of abuse.

The fear of being alone can be easy to spot in a potential victim. People with this kind of fear tend to exude some desperation level at the beginning of relationships, and they can sometimes come across as clingy. While ordinary people may think of being clingy as a red flag, manipulative people will see it as an opportunity to exploit somebody. If you are attached to them, they'll use manipulative techniques to make you even more dependent on them. They can withhold love and affection (e.g., by using the silent treatment) to make the victim fear that he/she is about to get dumped so that they act out of desperation and cede more control to the manipulator.

The fear of being alone is, for the most part, a social construct, and it disproportionately affects women more than men. For generations, our society has taught women that their goal in life is to get married and have children, so even the more progressive women who reject this social construct are still plagued by social pressures to adhere to those old standards. That being said, the fact is that men also tend to be afraid of being alone.

People with abandonment issues stemming from childhood tend to experience the fear of loneliness to a higher degree. There are also those people who may not necessarily fear loneliness in general, but they are afraid of being separated from the important people in their lives. For example, many people stay in abusive or dysfunctional relationships because they are afraid of being separated from their children.

Fear of Disappointing Others

We all feel a certain sense of obligation towards the people in our lives, but some are extremely afraid of disappointing others. This kind of fear is similar to the fear of embarrassment and the fear of rejection because it means that the person puts a lot of stock into how others perceive them. The fear of disappointing others can occur naturally. It can be useful in some situations; parents who are afraid of disappointing their families will work harder to provide for them. Children who are afraid of disappointing their parents will study harder at school. In this case, the fear is constructive. However, it becomes unhealthy when directed at the wrong people or when it forces you to compromise your comfort and happiness.

When manipulators find out that you fear disappointing others, they'll try to put you in a place where you sense as you owe them something. They'll do certain favors for you, and then they'll manipulate you into believing that you have a sense of obligation towards them. They will then guilt you into complying with any request whenever they want something from you.

Chapter 4. Strategies for Seduction, a Person with Manipulation

Seduction and sexual conquest are sometimes common features of dark psychology. They will show up so often that we will devote this guide to them and how they work. This is an important topic to discuss because all of us have been or know someone who has been seduced by someone else who used these dark psychological principles.

The human sex drive can be a very powerful urge, and not being able to fulfill it can sometimes lead to unhappiness, worry, and stress in a person's life. On the other side of things, some of the most famous historical figures are known for their frequent and full fulfillment of sexual urges. For example, emperors and kings have often been afforded the finest women as their reward just because of their status.

One very famous example is the powerful seducer King Henry the 8th from England. His women's appetite was so strong that he decided to create a new religion in his country to change his wife and marry any woman he chose. He also exercised utter control over all the wives he had, and many of them were beheaded when they didn't satisfy his needs or help him meet his goals any longer.

This begs the question: is all seduction a form of dark psychological seduction? Of course not! Yes, all seduction is going to involve the perusal of the other person. Those who don't have the skills of dark manipulation will clumsily do this. This is shown in some of the popular romantic comedies that come out, where the clumsy guy keeps making mistakes when they try to pursue the girl.

But a dark seducer will be someone who knows what they want and knows how to get it. They will go after the other person to fulfill their personal needs, and they often don't care how the other person feels about it. They can be charming, and they are not going to be clumsy at all, and they always know the right thing to say and do.

Why Do People Choose Dark Psychological Seduction?

One question that people will have is: why would someone want to choose this path for attraction? Isn't a better idea to go on some dates and court someone in an honest manner?

A dark seducer doesn't want to get into a relationship, at least not into the boring stuff with it. They want to just get certain things out of the area of romance. They don't care about the other person because they know they can use dark psychology techniques to find another partner if this one goes south. This allows them to approach life, and the relationship, with a non-needy and carefree mindset. If the seducer does decide to settle down with someone, they will be able to do it without feeling like they rushed or settled into the first relationship to get what they want.

So, how is a dark seducer have so much success and influence within the world of dating? They understand the dark psychology principles and have the right skills to execute these principles.

One of the key advantages that dark psychology users will have over their rivals, especially in dating, is that they understand the human mind, almost like a secret weapon. While others may feel like the human mind is impossible to understand, the dark seducer can read it like a book and get the information they want.

Someone who works on the principles behind dark psychology in the dating world may find that it will change their dating experiences compared to their past efforts. They will have a feeling of confidence and control, rather than feeling doubtful, needy, and insecure.

Sure, it may seem kind of mean. The dark seducer can jump from one partner to another, using each one in the manner that matters most to the seducer. Some people are harmed in this process, especially those looking for more of a long-term relationship or looking for more out of it.

But a dark seducer is only interested in what matters to them and nothing else. They can read the mind of their victim and be the exact person that the victim wants. However, they only do this to get their foot in the door and get what they want. As soon as the victim isn't meeting the seducer's needs, then the seducer will move on.

Where Does Dark Seduction Begin?

Now that we have an idea of dark seduction basics, it is time to move into how this seduction can work. Most dark seducers are going to have a guiding approach that is going to motivate their efforts. They will also have tactics that are going to come from their philosophy. Let's look at some of the different philosophies that a dark seducer may choose to use.

One approach is the deployment of a process that is rigid and structured. These seducers feel that they have mapped out how the sequence of attraction should be in great detail, and they may have a process that seems like it is from a flowchart. They want their seduction process to be replicable and predictable. These systems work for the dark seducer and work for others who understand these systems and learn how to implement them correctly.

These seducers are going to use a series of stages in their process. They will try to get the target to go through a range of emotions. This range is designed by the seducer to fit their own needs. They will move them through emotions such as interest, attraction, and then excitement. These seducers will see the whole process as a series of checkpoints that they need to pass through to help them reach their goals.

This method's strength is that it gives the dark seducer a feeling of certainty because they know the exact steps to take each time. They won't have any surprises that come up during the seduction, and it kind of becomes routine and habitual for the seducer. The biggest problem with this is that it doesn't consider that sometimes people will be unpredictable and won't go along with the structured emotional program that the seducer planned out.

Another option is the natural approach. This approach will involve the dark seducer cultivating a natural emotional state internal to the seducer and then expressing them freely to the one they are working to seduce. An example of this is when a person who uses this, is likely to spend some time trying to understand their own emotions and then try to perfect these. They are then going to express these to others. The philosophy behind this one is that "I can't make others feel good until I can feel good."

You can also work with hypnotic and Neuro-Linguistic Programming (NLP) seduction. NLP is a combination of neurological processes, language, and behavior. This is kind of a subset of dark seduction. Unlike the structured seduction that we talked about before or even the natural version, NLP and hypnotic seduction involve triggering specific emotional states in the victim and then linking these back to the seducer.

Let's look at an example of this. The NLP approach to seduction involves allowing people to explore their own intense positive emotions. The seducer may even try to get more of those emotions out. Then, they will work to anchor these to the seducer. That way, when the victim sees the seducer, they will naturally feel intense physical pleasure, even though they may not know why that happens.

Hypnotic seduction is another option to work with, but it can be difficult to work with regularly. This is because a few things will make someone suspicious about a seducer than the odd techniques that come with NLP. The other seduction types seem somewhat normal to the victim, but hypnotic seduction doesn't seem this way. However, some will respond to it.

Dark seduction can allow the seducer the ability to get exactly what they want out of the relationship. Those who are not looking to take advantage of others, but who are open about what they are doing and just use the techniques to give them more confidence and avoid a boring relationship can sometimes use it. However, there are plenty of dark seducers who use it as a way to use the other person, with no care about how it is going to affect the other person at all. Either way, it is still important to be on the lookout for this kind of behavior to not get into a bad relationship for you or isn't what you are looking for from the other person.

Chapter 5. Covert Emotional Manipulation

Covert emotional manipulation is an exceptional phenomenon that can happen to anybody, even you. Behind the intensity of your mindfulness alertness is where emotional manipulation operates and restrains you emotionally, while as a victim, you know nothing about what is happening.

A skillful emotional manipulator will do to you to influence you to place into their hands all your sensitive safety and senses of self-worth. Manipulators will continually and methodically break off your self-esteem and identity until there is little left the instant you make such a severe miscalculation.

Psychopaths and manipulators manipulate much in the same way as "pick-up artists" and narcissists. As for psychopaths, they have a perception that they are in charge and look down at others as their game to suit their hunting needs. Psychopaths have no compassion, no remorse or guilt, no conscience, and no ability to love. Achieving anything they want, including money, sex, or influence and taking control and power, is a game of manipulators. Not only that, but psychopaths also destroy their victims psychologically, emotionally, physically, and spiritually in the course of their actions. They use all tactics to realize their wishes. They will get going to the next conquest after they have won the game, filled with contempt for you and getting bored.

Covert manipulators cannot have a genuine connection even though they are so smart. They have a strategy from the beginning. Apart from that, they are proficient at reading your mind. Gaining knowledge of your strengths, weaknesses, dreams, fears, and desires is so easy for them. With an armory of valuable manipulation schemes that they have chosen carefully and personalized only for you, it is not for them to hesitate to use all these against you. They yearn for control and power and will always persist to control you, even if it results in harming you.

At a point when you think your life has got the blessing of a tender bond through the magical excitement that has made a comfortable and delightful appearance, it might be that something quite sinister and different is behind it. To conceal their exact strategy and personalities is one of the skills of manipulators. The main goal of these psychopaths is to fool you into trusting that they love and ready to do anything for you so you can confide in them in the course of a frenzied process of passionate illusion. They craft this stage of deep attachment to pin you and make you susceptible to the abuse and manipulation that will ensue.

After a while, demeaning will replace loving. From then on, degrading will follow, and manipulators will confuse, exploit, and diminish your self-worth, self-esteem, and self-respect. To keep you eager to do anything to save the relationship and to let you hold yourself responsible for not cherishing a great relationship and vouching to save the affair no matter what, manipulators will make a pleasant appearance as loving individuals that hook you.

To show your devotion to the relationship, you will be eager to acknowledge sheer morsels. You won't have any thought of talking about your emotions, fears, and needs, which is not the psychopath's concern and consider unacceptable weaknesses. When things go wrong, you will shift the blame on yourself, analyzing every mood and every word, becoming quite confused about what is happening, and recalling the conversations. Your life or job will suffer and your dealings with other people and your mental and physical health.

Your manipulator will try to have you with them, waiting for the time you become a hopeless disaster. At that point, they will let you know with seething contempt and disdain how they are bored with you and don't want you anymore. They will then leave you a sensitive mess who wonders just what happened to your life, speculating your perfect affair crumbled into the gulf of hell from heaven-on-earth.

Struggling with feelings of acute emotional grief and confusion comes to all preys of this deceptive and underhanded manipulation. Many of them also experience rage, obsessive thoughts, insomnia, misplaced self-esteem, panic, anxiety, inability to trust, poor health, fear, use of drugs or alcohol, and absence of support. Sometimes, extreme and irrational behavior can happen, including withdrawal and isolation from family, friends, and society. Suicidal actions or thoughts are part of what most victims face.

The question is, do these manipulators truthfully want love in the first place? Maybe they never have any desire for love. In a situation such as this, the purpose is that of victimization. The manipulator would have had their target plans when they discovered that you are open to their advances.

On the other hand, the occasion might end up badly even if the manipulator has a real attraction for you. Because it is the incentive scheme of the brain, things and people stimulate and excite these people. In fact, for those with features of psychopathy, the system works quite well. Indeed, studies have found that far from that of an average individual, manipulators' reward system is more sensitive. Consequently, it is with the intensity that they establish a relationship.

A Deeper Look at Manipulation Tactics

Covert manipulative individuals make use of tactics to accomplish two things simultaneously:

- Conceal their intention

- Invite you to fear, doubt, and concede

Tactics that are generally the most effective in manipulating other people, especially neurotics, are a few tactics covert manipulative people use more frequently. The key to personal empowerment is to know how to deal with these manipulation methods when you recognize them.

With just about any behavior imaginable to accomplish their aims, it is amazing how capable the more skilled manipulators can be. Armed with these tactics, manipulators will thoroughly evaluate how they will manipulate their target character when the manipulators know their victim inside out and are familiar with their target's fears, sensitivities, conscientiousness level, core beliefs, and so much more. Moreover, in a covert war of dominance, manipulators will have a considerable prospect making way for them to use that person's traits, especially their most collectively attractive characteristics, against them.

It will be appropriate for us to focus our attention on the more conventional approaches they employ and give in-depth details on why the tactics are so efficient. It is not realistic to talk about different feasible behaviors covert manipulators can use to influence another person. Having a good understanding of the fundamentals of manipulation works will reinforce your insight into the various potential tactics manipulators might apply and give you superior conscious control of the nature of upsetting encounters with all manipulators.

There is a rationalization tactic, which we may call "justifying", or "excuse-making." Originated from the Freudian notion, the word rationalization indicates that, on occasion, against the fear they might have suffered by engaging in dealings that damage their principles, people defend themselves unaware. They will assuage any qualms of conscience when they find reasons that appear to make their achievement more benign, appropriate, understandable, and acceptable. However, the assumption for this situation implies that the person has a highly sensitive conscience, and this type of rationalization is a mostly unconscious process and strictly internal.

Manipulators know what they are doing when they make explanations for their actions in some situations. When this set of people is looking to validate themselves, they certainly have obvious intention in mind. They use this approach when they know that they plan to do something or have done something most people would regard as wrong. However, manipulators stay determined to do it even when they know it is wrong and how their actions negatively represent them. They have permission to do it, such as the aggressive characters' situation or the case of more self-absorbed individuals, or they may clash against the accepted rules.

Most essential to identify is that at the time, manipulators are justifying their actions; they are neither unconsciously fending off any anxiety nor defending. Instead, they are actively at war against a set of standard manipulators who know society wants them to accept. More importantly, they are also attempting to get your support. Unlike open defiance, undercover manipulators prefer this type of tactic because it not only helps to mask their manipulative goals and various revealing parts of their personality, but at the same time helps them to preserve a more positive social image by making someone else identify with the supposed rationality of their actions or have a similar perception to their own. When the person accepts their premise with this strategy, the door of wielding the mutual domination and contest of image is opening gradually.

It is not that manipulators don't understand that their actions are wrong or that most people would see them as evil; instead, they hate your negative appraisal of their personality and perhaps end any relationship with them. More importantly, they should not engage in such behavior again because covert manipulative people don't want to incorporate and allow. Even when they still apply the tactic, they oppose a standard and hold up the inculcating that standard into their social ethics. It is the visible signal that they can engage in a similar activity in any related situation.

Now, let us talk about denial, another tactic. Denial is a word that had its origin from the psychology of Freudian. Freud invented it as an unconscious and primitive resistance against intolerable emotional pain. With other tactics such as pretending that they are innocent, manipulators often will use denial. This situation is when someone you have confronted acts as if they know nothing of what you are saying or they pretend in a vain way that they did nothing of which to be guilty or ashamed. They will often use faking gullibility and denial with such apparent confidence and intensity that you start to be curious about your sanity and perception. That moment, you start out knowing that you have caught them on the action, and one way or another, using this tactic, you begin to wonder if you are making any sense at all. This tactic is quite an efficient one-two manipulation blow!

However, the main missiles in the arsenal of any manipulator are the strategy of guilt-tripping and shaming. The fact behind this analysis is that precision defines the high degree of neurotics and cannot stand thinking that their actions are shameful or wrong. As a result, making them believe that what they have done should make them feel ashamed or guilty is the perfect way to control them. Conscientious individuals sometimes attempt to shame or guilt on their prey, hoping that it will somehow induce their behavior.

Covert is when an attempt is made to communicate with the subject's unconscious mind without knowing that they will be put through hypnosis. It comprises a string of techniques such as conversational hypnosis or NLP (neuro-linguistic programming), body language, and other powerful communication and interaction strategies.

Chapter 6. Covert Manipulation in a Love Relationship

The love-bombing is hard to ignore. They will make you feel like you are the most important person in the world to them, and you will be showered with loving gestures such as poems, love letters, gifts, or just merely the fact that they always have time for you.

The first few times they overreact to something, you might be able to justify it in your mind. There is a simple stage in a relationship where a kiss and a few sappy words can fix any argument.

A narcissist cannot have a productive argument. When people in a healthy and loving relationship disagree, their goal is to learn how to communicate better and find out where the miscommunication happened this time. When it is narcissistic abuse, they want to demean and shame you.

It is one that is void of name-calling and hurling accusations at one another. An argument is also not the time to bring up past grievances. This is sometimes referred to as the "kitchen sink" method. This is a very unhealthy way of arguing, but one that is often used by narcissists. They mean to make you feel like a wrong person.

They will not hear you out if you come to them with a concern about how they treat you. They will say something like, "do you think you're perfect?" This focuses the attention away from what they have done that is hurtful to you. For example, you might tell them you don't want them to call you names. Their response is, "You're not always a ray of sunshine around me either." In this situation, they did not hear you out at all. They shut down what you were trying to say to them.

A narcissist's first impulse will always be to self-protect. They are not interested in listening to your point of view, nor do they want to reach a compromise. They want to make sure they do not have any tarnishes on their character. That is because if they are not flawless, they are worthless. That is their thought process. This is most likely because, during childhood, they were only given praise when they succeeded.

The covert narcissist will be honest with you about what their grievances are in a relationship. Instead, they will go to other people. There will often be a cheating situation that arises, but they will rally many people against their partner. They often aim to taint their mutual friends' idea of them.

Venting to a confidant such as a best friend or family member is alright and something you will need to do at times. Speaking ill of your partner is not. When you come to a confidant with a legitimate issue, you still want to preserve the relationship's integrity. This is because you are talking to someone outside of the situation and will not share what you say with other people.

While communicating with your partner is essential, you sometimes need to express that would only harm the other person. It is okay to have things to say that you don't want your partner to hear. Where it becomes morally grey is when a person consistently goes to people outside of the relationship with the intent of bashing their significant other.

There is a difference between venting and bashing. While harsh words may be said when a person is venting, they still value the other person. As humans, we will get frustrated with one another, especially if we have an intimate relationship, which will inevitably come with miscommunications and disagreements.

This is an example of venting: "It hurts my feelings when they talk on the phone at the dinner table. It makes me feel like they would rather spend their free time talking to other people besides me." On the other hand, this is bashing "They're impossible to live with. They're always on the phone, ignoring me. I always try so hard, and they never give anything in return."

In the first example, the person is expressing frustrations but not talking about the person negatively or aiming to damage their reputation. In the second example, the language is inflammatory, and it hints toward a deep resentment towards the other person.

"You always" and "you never" are terms narcissists use in arguments.

Narcissists are infamous for their jealousy. They call every interaction you have with everyone in your life, particularly towards the gender you prefer, into question. You can never reassure them enough that you are not going to leave them for someone else. Acting jealous is designed to isolate you. Everything and everyone in your life makes them feel threatened.

Jealousy is not cute. It does not mean your partner is so in love with you that it hurts them to see you talking to someone else. It might sound very romantic when they word it like that, and it might make you feel loved, but what it means is that they want ownership of you.

It is crucial to remember to keep your priorities straight when you begin college. They are trying to put pressure on you to prove to them that you are faithful to them, which will mean your attention is divided while trying to navigate through the complex environment that is college.

A jealous person will call often and want to have long conversations. You cannot do this and study at the same time. Anyone who makes you feel like you need to choose between them and pursuing your education and the things that will further your career is not suitable for your life. They might tell you that you never loved them in the first place if you choose your education, but they did not put you first if they made you feel like you need to limit yourself to keep them.

This leads to another thing a narcissist does in a relationship. They give ultimatums. They will say, "okay, fine, you either stop going to that class or we're breaking up. It's your choice!" This may sound extreme, but that is how unreasonable the demands of a narcissist will become. They will say it's your choice, but it is a threat.

Covert narcissists harbor resentments indefinitely. They might say the conflict is over, and they have moved past it, but if you do something to cause them narcissistic injury, you will hear about it again in perpetuity. This is where a double standard in the relationship begins. They can say and do extremely rude and hurtful things to you, and they will expect you to forgive them after giving you a half-hearted non-apology.

If you are in a relationship with a narcissist, you will often be compared unfavorably to other people. You will be told that you are much more difficult to get along with than these people. This is because, at their core, a narcissist has a very juvenile mentality. They want what is most beneficial to them at the moment. They also do not understand why everyone else seems to be so much easier to get along with than their partner.

They do not live with these other people who seem so shiny. They only see them when they are at their best, and when they spend time with them, it is the good times: for example, it is a neighborhood get-together, and everyone is dressed their best. Drinks are being poured, and food is on the grill. Everyone is laughing and talking, and when the party is over, everyone leaves. All the cleanup is left to the people who hosted the party. We see every side of our spouses or significant others. We only see a certain depth of our acquaintances. You will have much fewer and less intense conversations with those you don't see as often.

They look at people they only see once in a while and then compare them to the person they live with and therefore see every day in every state, even the least glamorous ones. They might be married and even have children with this person. Marriage is difficult even when the relationship is healthy, especially when children come into the equation. Now, not only are you trying to navigate through life between just the two of you, but now you are both responsible for the life, growth, and well-being of other people.

When you share responsibilities this great with someone, you are not always at your best with each other. When you have financial troubles or one of the children begins to act up, tempers will be short, and arguments will be more often. When you compare two relationships, one complex where you share marriage and children, and another relationship where you only see each other when both are well. Your partner will come out, not seeming as good as the other person. Narcissists also do not think about what habits they have that might be unappealing to their partner. They do not consider the idea that they might not be easy to live with themselves.

A narcissist does not consider these factors when they discard one romantic partner to start a relationship with another person.

While they are unfaithful to their partner, they are also rude to them. This makes their partner feel completely unmotivated to try to be attractive or be intimate with them. They talk to this person like a dog and fantasize about how much better life would be cheating. They think about how much more fun they have with this person. They believe their partner is no fun, and the person they see in secret is so much more exciting than them.

Chapter 7. How the Mind Works When It Is Manipulated?

When it comes to working with dark manipulation, there will be many different methods and techniques that we can use to get what you want. Remember, we are talking about some forms of manipulation that will help us get what we want but may harm the other person in the process. This means that they may not be seen as the best options to work with, and you may feel a bit uncomfortable with them if you have not worked in dark manipulation, or even with dark persuasion, in the past.

However, working with these techniques will help you to get the results that you want. They will ensure that the other person you are using as your target will be likely to do the actions or say what you would like them to, even though it may not be in their best interests. With that said, let's take a look at some of the different dark manipulation tactics that you can use to get someone else to do what you want.

Using Isolation to Get What You Want

The first technique that can be used in mind control includes isolation. Humans are very social creatures. They like to spend some time talking with others, spending time out in public, having close friends and family, and spending time in more social situations. When we take this social aspect away from many individuals, it changes how they look at life.

Complete physical isolation can be the most powerful. This is when the subject is taken away from all contact with others, including email, social media, phone calls, and physical contact. This is something that has been seen in cults and with other groups. They will often take the person far away from others, and then the only human contact that the person can have is with the captors.

This total physical isolation can be really hard to do, and it is usually only done in really intense situations. If you are just trying to use manipulation, you usually don't want to go through and completely isolate the target. However, it is common for a manipulator to try to attempt their target mentally as much as possible.

There are many methods that the manipulator can use to get what they want with the help of manipulation. They could include some seminars that last a week and isolate them from what they usually do. They could be many criticisms of the person's family and close friends so that the target feels bad and stops seeing them. It could be jealousy that keeps the target at home and limits the influence that anyone outside the manipulator has on the person.

Once the manipulator can control the information that goes to the target, they can share information, withhold information, and do anything that they would like to continue influencing the target as much as they would like. The target will become reliant on the manipulator, and this is how the manipulator can work and get what they want from the target. There are no outside influences to tell the target that something is wrong or watch out, ensuring the target even more.

Criticism

The option to work with when it comes to manipulation is the idea of using criticism. This one is sometimes used with isolated or on its own, and it works well because it makes the target feel like they are always doing something that is wrong and that they cannot meet the high standards of the manipulator. The criticism can always show up on various topics and could include how they look, who they hang out with, their clothes, their beliefs, and anything that the manipulator thinks will work for this.

When a manipulator decides to use this tactic, they will be good at hiding it behind one of their compliments to the other person. Alternatively, they will say something nice and add this little jab at the end of it. This allows them to say all the mean things they want, and then they can say that the target misheard or misunderstood them and that they hadn't meant any harm by it. This puts the target in a bad spot because they know the manipulator is mean to them, but they are the ones who look paranoid and bad in this situation.

The criticism that the manipulator is going to use is often going to be small. They don't want to start out using really big criticisms that are obvious because the target doesn't want to be criticized. If the manipulator starts with something big, the target is going to fight back and walk away. However, when it starts small with some little comments along the way, it starts to plant a bit of self-doubt, something that the target will notice, but they often are not going to fight back against.

They will start with something that may seem like a compliment or like that will sound like they are helpful, but they are trying to be hurtful in the process in reality. They may say something like, "I didn't know that you liked the color blue. I think you should go with something else." This one will have the hidden meaning inside it that you don't look good in what you are wearing, and your clothes don't look that well.

Or maybe you bring in your favorite outfit to a meeting to make yourself feel better. You are excited and feel good about how you look and feel in the outfit, but then they are going to say something about how they liked you in some other outfit better. It isn't necessarily mean, but it is said in a manner and at a time that it ends up hurting your feelings in the process.

As time goes on, the type of criticism that is going to be used against the target is going to get worse. Moreover, the criticism will become quite a bit more obvious and add in a bit more self-doubt here. This will make it so that the target starts to rely on the manipulator a bit more. This is since the target will feel like they have so many flaws that are hard to ignore and that the only person who can like them and maybe even loves them through these flaws will be the manipulator. The fact that the manipulator is still around is a good sign that they care, which causes the target to be more willing to do what the manipulator asks.

The manipulator will find that they can use this criticism more of us against them if it works better. They could even choose to move their criticism against the outside world to claim they are superior.

When this happens, the manipulator will claim to their target that they are super lucky that the manipulator is even associating with them. The manipulator will ensure that they are important so that the target is more likely to stick around and do what they want. This alone is meant to be enough if it is done in the right manner so that the target feels lucky just because the manipulator is going to spend time with them.

Alienating the Target to Get What They Want

No one wants to be alienated. They want to feel like they are a part of the group. They want to feel accepted, as they belong, and more. This is never more apparent than when we see a newcomer. When someone is new to town, or to school, to work, or somewhere else, you will notice that they are trying to figure out how to join the group and get them to accept them. They are worried that they will be alienated, and to avoid this, they will do everything to get others to like them and go along with them, which is where the manipulator can come in and get what they want.

Newcomers who start to join a new manipulative group are usually going to receive a very warm welcome. And they will form many new friendships that seem to be much deeper and have a lot more commitment and meaning behind them compared to anything that they were able to experience in the past.

There are several reasons for this one. First, this gets the target to feel welcome and more indebted to the group and the manipulator. They are thankful that they have these deep connections, and it is usually easier to get a friend to go along with something that a stranger, so it works to the benefit of the manipulator. Add in that the target is scared to be alienated, then they are going to do what they can to keep the relationships going strong.

Simply because we do not want to be taken away from the crowd and don't want others to have anything to do with us, we will do what the manipulator wants us to. The fact that humans are very social creatures and like to be included in some kind of group all of the time, it is likely that we are going to give in to these urges to do what the manipulator wants, even if we don't feel like it is the best thing for us.

Using Social Proof as a Form of Peer Pressure

We like it when we can be a part of the group. Sometimes we center this around wanting to fit in, and we will follow the rules and do what we can to make sure that we are liked and part of the group. Even when we are more introverted and don't want to be in the group all of the time, we still want to find a group of people we can be around and fit in.

Chapter 8. Hypnosis

Hypnosis is a state of mind that individual's fall into where they are no longer in control of their actions. This is often done in therapeutic circumstances to help individuals find the peace they need within themselves to confront their deepest and darkest traumas. Hypnosis also offers a means to persuade and influence others.

Hypnosis and mind control may seem like the same thing since they involve exerting control over someone else. However, there are glaring contrasts between the two. To recognize the distinctions, you must become more acquainted with what they depend on.

Hypnosis is an artificially induced condition in which the individual reacts to inquiries or prompts from the hypnotist. The procedure can be used on an individual or a gathering of people for a specific reason. At the point when this is utilized for therapeutic purposes, the process is known as hypnotherapy. In any case, when it is being used as a type of diversion for a crowd of people, it tends to be alluded to as organized hypnosis.

Then again, personality control is the way toward utilizing a few traps in getting the ideal response you need from others. You can use the secret to get aggregate or fractional command over what is happening in someone else's psyche.

When it is utilized amid reflection, it can enable you to center around your examination subject.

You can deal with your feelings and contemplations when you participate in this sort of reflection. As a rule, incredible people who accomplished extraordinary life achievements could have excellent command over their psyches through daily reflection.

Having seen the essential meanings of hypnosis and mind control, it is obvious to pinpoint their disparities. The real contrast you'll see between these two is that hypnosis must be utilized on others. It is doubtful that there is any method by which you can hypnotize yourself. A subliminal specialist is necessary to induce hypnosis.

Then again, personality control reflection can be utilized on oneself just as on others. You can, without much of a stretch, take part in this sort of contemplation anytime. All you need is to find a tranquil spot, take a seat, and afterward think. You can influence others to concur with you on specific focuses using mind control traps.

Once more, another distinction is seen in the manner in which hypnosis is connected with mind control. In case you are having an issue of fear, smoking, or appetite, a trance specialist can enable you to opt-out if the hypnosis was done with the correct mindset at heart.

Sometimes, the hypnosis specialist may utilize a few methods in reflection to get individuals to be comfortable with capturing the reaction they need at a specific point in time. It is highly unlikely you can utilize mind control traps to spellbind somebody. It is intended for strategic purposes.

Hypnosis and mind control have clear contrasts. A few components utilized in one may likewise be used in the other, but they are not the same. Everything relies upon how you are ready to draw in the essential standards included.

Hypnosis includes two principal components: acceptance and proposals. Trancelike acceptance is the major proposal conveyed amid the hypnosis; however, it should comprise a matter of discussion.

Proposals are commonly communicated as suggestions that inspire automatic reactions from the members, who don't trust they have much control over the circumstance. A few people are likewise more susceptible than others, and specialists have discovered that they are more likely to have a decreased feeling of authority while under hypnosis.

Susceptibility to hypnosis has been characterized as the capacity to encounter proposed modifications in physiology, sensations, feelings, musings, or conduct. Neuroimaging procedures have demonstrated that these individuals show higher activity levels in the prefrontal cortex, the foremost cingulate cortex, and the mind's parietal systems amid various hypnosis periods.

These are regions of the mind associated with a scope of complex capacities, including memory and observation, feelings, and assignment learning. Be that as it may, the particular cerebrum components associated with hypnosis are as yet hazy. However, researchers are starting to sort out the neurocognitive profile of this procedure.

How would you know whether somebody has been hypnotized? Various changes indicate that the subject is in a hypnotic trance. NLP calls these profound daze markers, and they are a set of highly detailed observations one can make of the subject. Recognizing such markers requires practice and focus. Not all of these markers need to be present to establish that a subject is under hypnosis.

Hypnotic Strategies

The first step in putting someone in a hypnotic state is opening the individual's mind to suggestion. The hypnosis specialist uses a vast range of techniques and, depending on the specialist's skill and the susceptibility of the subject. The outcome may vary.

Hypnosis by relaxation is one of the most common methods of hypnosis. Have you ever heard a hypnosis specialist ask an individual to make him or herself as comfortable as possible? By doing this, the person being hypnotized falls into a relaxing state where the mind tends to shut down on immediate surroundings.

Here are some basic techniques for unwinding:

- Relax your body and mind
- Settle down
- Count in receding order in your mind
- Control what your body and mind is thinking and doing
- Feel your muscles give in to relaxation
- Tone down your voice to a whisper

The handshake strategy for hypnotism involves a hypnosis expert shaking an individual's hand. However, where you might think this is a usual way for the public to greet or welcome each other, hypnosis specialists use this for another advantage.

Instead of just shaking your hand, they will grab, twist your wrist, or pull you forward towards them, so you become unstable. When you are unstable in that split second, the perfect opportunity arises for a hypnosis specialist to control your mind.

Eye prompts can also be important in hypnosis. Talking to someone, it is only natural for one's eyes to wander to surroundings or perhaps a glimpse of something in the distance. A hypnosis specialist will take note of this and, within a short period, learn what prompts you to move your eyes left, right, up, or down. With that, they gain access to the way you think, feel, and respond to certain things surrounding you.

Another approach for the hypnosis of others includes mesmerizing proposals that aren't always obvious suggestions. This kind of suggestion is proposed by the hypnotizer and involves something they wish the subject to do. These proposals also come after the customer has already fallen into more of a stupor.

This is when they are the most open to impact. Rather than telling the hypnotized to do something, the command is masked in a mystifying suggestion. If you want someone to sit down, you don't say, "Sit down," you might say, "You should take a minute to relax in the chair over there."

One method you can do to help improve your hypnotic tactics is to record yourself doing hypnosis and listen to it. If you can fully hypnotize yourself, you can be assured you will have the skills to do this to others. Start by listening to other hypnosis recordings and determine which methods have managed to work best on you.

After this, you can write your original script. Remember, never hypnotize someone who doesn't consent to it. Hypnosis helps the other person find a state of relaxation while also helping to persuade them to do something healthy or beneficial.

Like NLP, all of these methods take practice to master. Don't be discouraged because you cannot hypnotize someone else the first time you try fully. Take note of each hypnosis session that you have, as well. What about it worked once that didn't work as well the next time?

Remember not to use information gained from another in a hypnotic state against them either. Sometimes, they might fall into such a stupor that they become in a dreamlike state. They might say something they don't fully mean, much like a person on pain medication after getting their wisdom teeth removed might.

In contrast to manipulation, these skills are intended to be used for good purposes, as well. You might find it becomes easy to hypnotize others once you have practiced, but your motivation shouldn't be primarily for your gain. There are benefits that both you and the entranced can gain from your hard-earned skill. However, you choose to use these powerful methods, along with the NLP tips, you can be helpful and empowering to both you and the person you can influence.

Understand that when you agree to hypnotize someone else, you are also given a certain responsibility. They are trusting you with a vulnerable headspace that they probably would not entrust to just anyone. Once you attempt to persuade someone, you agree to accept any negative outcomes due to your influence.

The healthy, positive influence will take time to build, and that is true even when you are using these hypnotic techniques. To have long-lasting persuasion that will benefit all parties is a great privilege, and it is up to you to find a positive way to utilize this power.

Chapter 9. Office Politics or Sociopathic Tricks? – The Workplace Manipulators

The workplace is a fertile ground for the manipulation of various types to occur. Many people will find they encounter at least several of the following types of workplace manipulators throughout their careers. It can be tough to know how to draw the line between normal workplace politics, gossip and banter, and actual manipulation. Classifying some of the main types of manipulators within the world of work can help potential targets stay away from the wrong type of colleague before finding their world turned upside down and their professional life damaged beyond repair.

The Blackmailer

The Blackmailer is a type of workplace manipulator that can have a serious impact not only on their victims' careers but also on their mental wellbeing and overall sanity. The basic method of the blackmailer is to appear friendly and highly trustworthy at first. This is usually achieved by finding a newcomer to the workplace or someone who does not fit in with others particularly well.

Once an appropriate target has been identified, the blackmailer will invest a serious amount of time and effort to win over their target and deceptively earn their trust. This is often done by taking a new member of staff under their wing and offering to mentor them and make their new life at the company as easy as possible.

The blackmailer will often form friendships with their intended target that occurs outside of work and inside work. This is essential for the blackmailer's manipulation to be effective. It must involve the target seeing the blackmailer more as a trusted friend than simply as a colleague.

Over time, the blackmailer will begin to elicit sensitive information from their target subtly. This could involve controversial opinions about the other people that the two work with or even sensitive details of the victim's personal life, such as their sexual orientation or political views. The blackmailer will keep going until they feel they have accumulated sufficient information to use against their victim.

Once the blackmailer has some powerful information to hold against their target, such as a covert phone recording of them saying something disparaging, or a photograph of the target behaving controversially in some way, the blackmailer will begin to hold it against them. They may make threats such as planning to reveal sensitive information to others within the workplace or even the target's loved ones and family.

The blackmailer will often demand increasing money or favors from the victim to keep their secrets safe. The victim lives in a continuous state of fear as they do not know when and if they will have their secrets revealed. This has a destructive effect on the victim's mental health and can lead to breakdowns and major anxiety levels.

The False Ally

The false ally is a type of workplace manipulator who is skilled at hiding their true intentions. They will seem to be a keen ally of their target. They are likely to suggest that they go to big places in the workplace and support each other's climb up the career ladder.

The false ally will often begin by making an over the top show of helping out their intended target. This is designed to ensure that the target sees them as trustworthy figures and feels a debt of gratitude towards the false ally. Once the false ally feels they have earned the trust and respect of their target, they will begin to exert subtle levels of control over them.

Some typical plays in the playbook of the false ally include coercing a victim into acting in the ally's self-interest and not of the victim. This will usually take place under the guise of doing 'what's best for both of us' when it will be anything but. This type of manipulation is especially effective if the victim is naive and idealistic. The false ally can tap into the victim's desires and ambitions to gain their compliance in carrying out the false ally's bidding.

The endgame of the false ally is typically to see their career advance while their targets either stalls or are damaged irreparably. This often takes the form of the false ally gaining some form of recognition, like a promotion, at the target's expense, but due to the efforts and choices the target has been coerced into. Often, the victim has no knowledge that they have been played like a puppet until it is too late, and the false ally has already benefited.

The Abuser of Power

It is a well-known fact that power has the potential to corrupt human beings. The office is one of the most common arenas for such behavior to occur. The abuse of power can take many different forms, but they all involve someone unfairly wielding a position of hierarchical authority over another person.

Some common examples of power abuses include those in supervisory or management positions asking for inappropriate or over the top levels of support and compliance from those they have power over. This can take less serious forms, such as getting workers to put in hours that they are not paid for, or take more serious forms such as pressuring female employees into sexual liaisons to promise promotions and job security.

It is important to distinguish between someone who legitimately exerts power and someone who abuses it. To cross the line into the realms of covert emotional manipulation, it must fulfill the following criteria for the wielding of power to cross the line. Firstly, the manipulator must have authority over their targets, such as their manager or some other formal authority position. Secondly, the manipulator must use their power in a way that is intended to control their victim through the manipulation of their emotions. Abusers of power can draw on their victims' feelings of job insecurity or doubt about their future.

Abusers of power are particularly dangerous types of manipulators as they have very little chance of being caught. This is owed to the point that it can be difficult for someone to blame their boss or superior for their actions. Unless clear evidence exists, which is very rare to happen, it is likely to come down to the victim's word in contradiction of the manipulator's word. Sadly, this is rarely sufficient evidence for a company to take any action against the person who has abused the power they hold.

The Sexual Predator

Sexual predators can take the form of almost any other type of workplace manipulator and exist on their own. Simply put, a sexual predator seeks to act in an inappropriate sexual way towards someone they work with. This can range in severity.

At one end of the scale, workplace sexual predators may simply make another member of staff feel uncomfortable. This can be through looks, gestures, or inappropriate physical contact. Despite this being the mildest type of sexually predatory behavior that can occur, it is still unbelievably serious and should be avoided at all costs.

Sadly, many workplace sexual predators take things a lot further than merely making a victim feel uncomfortable. Many sexual predators will coerce their victims into carrying out a sexual nature that they feel pressured or forced into doing. To ensure that their victim stays quiet about what has occurred, the predator will often gather some kind of compromising evidence, such as photographs. The predator threatens to expose the victim's colleagues and family if they cause any predator problems.

Although many workplaces have policies intended to protect against any type of inappropriate sexual behavior in the workplace, they are rarely enough to stop the worst predators from going about their manipulation. This is owed to the fact that skilled predators of this nature can ensure they do not leave any evidence whatsoever. They are also likely to choose victims who have low self-esteem or have some other reason that makes them unlikely to tell others what has taken place.

The Bully

Bullies may seem to be a fairly trivial workplace manipulator, but this is far from the case. Bullying can severely impact someone's happiness and well-being. Is often hard to detect, and even harder to stop. This is owed to the detail that a skilled manipulator engaged in the practice of bullying is likely to mask their actions as friendship or advice underneath the friendly veneer. However, something far more dangerous and sinister is occurring. Bullying can range in severity. On one end of the scale, a bully may seem to be making jokes that just happen to involve the victim. However, this is not what is happening. What seems like a joke is often an attempt to gradually erode the victim's confidence and leave them vulnerable and doubtful. Cognitive dissonance is created in the victim's mind as, on the one hand, they are aware that the comments or actions of the bully are hurting them, but on the other, they do not want to appear overly sensitive or thin-skinned. This often results in the victim begrudgingly accepting the bullying taking place, even if it is hurting them in the long path. For bullying to work, the manipulator chooses their target carefully. They are likely to select someone who lacks self-confidence and is not particularly popular within the workplace. This is owed to the point that the victim will put up with the bullying, as it is often the only form of attention they have received in the workplace up until that point. Bullying can have severe consequences in the long run. It can chip away at the victim's confidence and happiness and, perversely, create a sense of dependency on the manipulator and the attention they provide. The effects can be with a victim for the rest of their life. They may have severe difficulty trusting another again and forming any type of healthy relationship in the future. This is because they will have fallen into the pattern of seeking approval and validation via negative attention.

Chapter 10. Human Behavior and Manipulation

Once you have gotten a decent read on a person, the step to mastering your environment and analyzing your potential in each situation is learning how to manipulate another person's feelings and reactions through subtler cues, both verbal and non-verbal. This will create an environment where your suggestions can thrive.

Don't beat yourself up for thinking outside the box when it comes to analyzing and influencing people. While some people might call it manipulation, you can simply tell them that you are extremely persuasive. What's more, there is nothing to say that the person you are influencing wasn't waiting for an excuse to move forward in the direction you suggested anyway. It is your creativity in constructing a good plan or formula that turns resistance into compliance.

Besides emotion, successful manipulation is all about the imbalance of power. There may be times when getting what you want from another person means using the home-court advantage, which means keeping the person in an environment where you have primary control. This includes your home, car, office, or even your side of town. This makes it harder for your target to do things such as dodge a conversation or even decide that they think they might hurt your feelings.

While it may seem surprising, letting people dominate the conversation is a good thing when you want to have the upper hand with them. You can establish their underlying weaknesses and strengths by listening to their stories and throwing in limited questions from time to time, which will also ingratiate you to them further. It makes you look as though you are supremely interested in what they have to say. However, you don't want the conversation to be one-sided, which means you want to tell them enough about your situation to make them feel comfortable, while at the same time hiding any information that weakens your point of view or that can be contorted to mean something else. Don't be afraid to lie to protect any weaknesses in your argument.

If someone is pushing you for more than they need, you can use a humble tone and explain that there are things about your no one would understand or that you aren't interesting enough to warrant talking about. This will make them curious, and it will also make them a little nurturing, which is where you can snag them. This is known as flipping the script, and it can be a very effective technique when used selectively.

Suppose you have to speak about facts and statistics. Ramble about as many as you can to be a bit overwhelming. At this time, you need to show interest in their part but establish that if you are to go along with whatever they are suggesting, you will have your own rules. Depending on the state you are currently in, this may be enough for them to "decide" to complete the task in question or give in to your suggestion because it is easier than going along with your stipulations.

Another way to manipulate a person is to change the modulation of your voice. If you are trying to intimidate a person, you will want to be loud. If you are seeking sympathy, lose the loud tone for a depressed, defeated tone instead. Most people are inclined to help a person who is feeling down. Now that you have their sympathy, ask for something. Suggest what you want in a way that seems impossible to achieve. Wait for their response, which should be some variation of, "I want to help you." Some people will want to offer up advice as a way to soothe you. To avoid losing control of the situation, you will need to consider their advice and find that their logic is faulty to ensure things remain under your control.

Manipulation Tools for Specific Situations

A key to pulling off any form of manipulation is to see what drives the person you are dealing with. For example, is it a religion? If so, you would need to focus on their devotion and find a creative way to get your point across using their religion. It is a good way to reinforce their opinion of themselves, most likely that they are godly and intelligent. As long as you focus on their utopian visions and aspirations, you will find this technique to be very effective.

Another tool that is useful from time to time is sarcasm. It allows you to express your discontent with someone while maintaining a doorway out as if you were just joking. However, be cautious, as sarcasm can be insulting and hurtful if misused. After you have been given a chance to vent, turn it around to the sarcastic "what if." This allows the person to hear your opinion, and it comes across like you are just defeated. Now they can save you. When they offer their help, humbly tell them it is not their responsibility, but that you need their support. It is helpful to add, "What would I do without you?"

You must keep in mind that you are being manipulated every day. The news, media, and those in power all deploy tactics to keep your attention or threaten your security for non-compliance. You are bombarded with images and stories that tug at your heart, anger your soul, and move you either into action or into seclusion. Just seeing how easily you can have the same effect on a person will allow you to recognize when it is being done to you. Awareness is life-changing. At this moment, you realize you have tried conventional methods of persuasion, being genuine and truly caring. Formerly, you got nothing in return, but you will from now on.

Be Creative

You will need to focus on your creativity for these manipulative tactics. Your goal is to transform someone's reality and alter their beliefs. Every situation is different, which means you will need to be creative and think on your feet. You must observe the cues a person is giving you. You must observe their reactions to you and others, as these can be very telling. Sometimes, just watching your target interact with others can give you more insight into how to manipulate them.

For example, if you see how a coworker reacted to a customer, you can use that to make them feel justified by adding your opinion to explain how they reacted. They will repeat the excuse you provided them. This can be used against them. If you are trying to get them to do something for you, just point out how they overreacted to that customer, which should shame them into following your suggestion. They should act in the way you suggest to minimize their past actions.

Sometimes all you have to do is create an image. Think of a spin on something that would suggest the person you are dealing with is a victim. Encourage them to see how others have been unappreciative and lazy compared to them. Suggest a course of action and reap the benefits.

If you are dying to know what someone feels about a situation, for example, in politics or religion, make up a story that you read on the internet that is sure to rile them up. Sit back, watch their reaction, and start agreeing with them. Be sure to add your perspective to draw them out of the shocking story into your plan. You might just be harvesting information to keep a profile on someone who is a threat to your vision of success. Building your profile, you will be able to understand their weakness in most situations.

Take Your Time

You can be sure to pay special attention to their strengths and find ways to undermine them. Don't proceed it so far as to where others observing can figure out what your intentions are, and instead always take the high road in public so that at the end of the day, most people will only ever see the public face you decide to show them.

Keep in mind that everyone just wants to be happy, which means they seek to understand and support people around them. They think it is rare for someone to take an interest in them without wanting something in return. This is where patience becomes your ally. You cannot act like someone has to be available at a moment's notice. Anyone can figure out that you have selfish motives if you display this impatient tendency. It might be killing you to lie in wait for the perfect opportunity, but it would kill you more to be seen as a fake. So, wait. Even encourage them to ask others about the situation. Once you have proven that you are only worried about them or want to see them succeed, then you can wiggle into their mind with subtle manipulation.

While playing on the heartstrings of another, you weaken their response. You cannot simply ignore that they might say no to your request or idea. You have to come across as genuine in trying to help or care about them. Find a way to make their "no" seem unreasonable without saying it directly. You will have to point out that if someone else acted as they did, they would see it as being stubborn or pig-headed with their closed mind. Let them know that the brain has a chemical response to doing something new and brave. Tell them that the brain lights up like a Christmas tree when changes are occurring.

The bottom line is that there is potential for manipulation. It is a creative process. It takes a little planning and observing, but if mastered, it can change your life. You will feel powerful every day. You will start to see every rejection as a canvas. It is your starting point. A word for word or gesture-by-gesture guarantee that you are in control.

Self-preservation is an important aspect of manipulation. You do not want to be perceived as a manipulator. You want to be known as the neutral person who sees all sides but uses logic to decide why your decision is more valid. Maintain a solid reputation for being thoughtful, and people will seek your opinion often. This is an advantage from the start. In a new group of people, you can find a way to agree with everyone and make a statement that you were always taught to show respect and think of all sides before making a decision.

Conclusion

Covert psychological manipulation is essential to the art of dark psychology. Many of the methods utilized with dark psychology will utilize this type of emotional manipulation, whether in part or entirely. As you learn a bit more about the world of dark psychology and its various symptoms, you will soon begin to see the signs of CPM. This is why it is so crucial to comprehend what CPM is precisely so that you can watch out for it in your daily life.

Covert psychological manipulation, or CPM, will attempt by a single person to attempt and influence the feelings and ideas of the other person in a manner that is considered deceptive and undiscovered by the one who is being manipulated. Being able to break down each of the words in CPM is very important to help you understand this subject's structures. Covert refers to the way that a manipulator can conceal their intentions. They wish to have the ability to hide the true nature of all their actions. Remember that not all types of influence and psychological manipulation will be classified as hidden. The victims of the concealed type, though, will usually not realize they are being controlled and will not have the ability to comprehend the way the manipulation is performed. Sometimes, they are not even able to look and determine the motivation of their manipulator.

This is why CPM is such a stealth bomber in the world of dark psychology. Its point is to prevent detection and defense up until it is far too late for the victim. The psychological side of the manipulator is going to be the specific focus of that manipulator. Other kinds of manipulation might include things like the other person's self-discipline, beliefs, and habits. Numerous manipulators will concentrate on this area of impact as they know that the other person's feelings are essential to the other elements of their character. Being able to manipulate the feelings of the other individual is essential. If a person has emotional control over the other individual, they will have complete control over them. The last piece of CPM is manipulation. It is typically thought that manipulation and impact are the same things. This is not true, though. Manipulation refers to the surprise and underhand process of influence outside the awareness of the one who is being controlled.

The objective behind this compared to someone who has the intent to influence can be a huge difference. They will enter into this with an influencer with the idea of "I wish to assist you in deciding that benefits you." With the manipulator, they have the thoughts of "I want to control you to supply advantage to myself secretly." As you can see, both of these are quite a bit different, so comprehending the objective behind any offered behavior is going to be a big part of choosing whether the scenario is hidden psychological manipulation or not.

Manipulative Circumstances

There are four primary situations in which CPM can take place. These consist of the household, romantic, individual, and professional parts of your life. Among the most typical kinds of CPM is romantic, and it can sometimes be the deadliest. There are some less obvious kinds of CPM that you can discover anywhere, and because they are less typical, they can often be the most unsafe. A good example of CPM is a managing romantic partner. If a woman remains in a relationship and her partner is trying to control her, she will be revolted by what is going on as soon as she figures it out. She might wish to discover a way to leave the circumstance. Thus, many times the controlling partner is going to exercise their impact as covertly as possible. They don't desire their partner to understand they are being managed, or the victim leaves, and there is nobody delegated control. If the manipulator achieves success, their spouse or sweetheart will continue to be a psychological manipulation victim. They might have difficulty recognizing that it is going on. This permits the manipulator to keep the control that they want with no danger of being found and losing the other person for good.

This can likewise occur with a buddy who would use CPM to get the outcomes they want when they have a relationship with another individual. In this group, one of the common types of manipulators will be covertly induced feelings of obligation, compassion, and guilt in a pal. The friend is being controlled in this way without understanding that they are being influenced. They may understand that they are acting differently to that buddy; however, they won't have the ability to explain why and how. You will discover that the expert part of your life can be another place for hidden emotional manipulators. Many people have worked for an employer or another person who had authority, who seems to set off some unidentified sensations of duty, worry, and regret in them.

Individuals who are manipulated in this manner might never identify why these feelings exist or where they come from, and in the world of CPM, the family can be the most troublesome. A proficient manipulator can discover a victim, even within their household, and the amount of influence they exercise can be dangerous. This is because the manipulator and the victim will have a very deep connection together. After all, they are related. When blood relations are included, the amount of influence and control can increase a fair bit. These family circumstances are so matched to utilizing CPM because most people currently feel a social responsibility to help their own family. They are willing to go a little more to guarantee the requirements of their family are addressed. Because of this predisposition, covert psychological manipulative practices will give you a malleable victim.

The (Bad) Love Giver

This consists of the severe, unforeseen, and robust expression of positive feelings towards a victim. It may, in the beginning, seem counterintuitive. Why do they behave so intensively positive at first if that individual is attempting to damage them? Since it matches its functions—that's why! This produces a deep sense of self-confidence, affection, and appreciation from a specific victim to their manipulator, and this is the principle behind love providing. Based on the manipulator's analysis, the degree to which enjoy providing is utilized, and the people on whom it is pre-owned forms the basis. A lonely, helpless victim who seeks help and consolation is most likely to be more love-bombed by the manipulator because the manipulator will know the victim will be more responsive to it. The more the victim is grounded, the less effort the manipulator will have to put into positivity. The meaning of the love giving technique offers two essential lessons on Emotional Manipulation. Firstly, the covert nature of Emotional Manipulation is well shown. Envision is trying to comprehend that love giving is an unfortunate thing. "Well, this guy was very sweet to me, and he made me feel very good." The red flags or warning signs of abuse are unlikely to be raised by such a declaration. This is a textbook example of how something can be provided as something favorable but has a negative result. The second general lesson pertinent to Emotional Manipulation that can be learned from love offering is how emotional manipulation is formed to suit every unique circumstance. Experienced manipulators have discreetly tested and learned from lots of encounters in their history. In any given scenario, you understand the strength and timing of each Emotional Manipulation strategy.

What is Empathy

Empathy is the capability to put yourself in another person's shoes and consider their emotions and sensations. An empath is an individual who can interact with others on several levels to experience their emotional wellness with precision. How empaths have this capacity has yet to be comprehended to many individuals, but numerous believe it is innate and transmitted through our DNA. As for how it runs, everything in deep space resonates with electrical energy; empaths are believed to can perceiving the shifts in the electrical energy around them. Empaths are usually considered compassionate, loving, sensitive to other individuals' feelings, and sympathetic. Would you be astonished to learn there's a dark side to being an empath? The essence of compassion itself makes sure that lots of are helped and supported by an empath. It likewise means empaths can see the world a lot more than we do, and as such, issues can happen in various areas of their lives. The dark side of empaths is that their sensations can't be managed. You might believe they are well versed in emotions, but the truth is they are in a constant fight to keep them under control. Sometimes, it can bring them down to depression since they so strongly feel others' feelings, specifically others' grief. They discover it difficult to separate their feelings and others and find other empaths to reveal their sensations. Empaths can accommodate a large amount of information from their sensitivity to electrical energy when managing negative energy resulting in fatigue. This can puzzle and exhaust them badly while attempting to understand everything. They are particularly prone to negative energy, as it greatly upsets them. They will easily end up being tired when all they can feel is negative energy. They are used by the less scrupulous amongst us because empaths are compassionate individuals who always believe in people's good nature. Empaths are generous and kind; they will attract only those who take and never return.

An empath can quickly fall under deep anxiety when they discover they have been conned. Because empathy tends to give to others instead of getting, it is most likely that they overlook their wellness, including their bodies and minds. This is the dark side all frequently since it's all too easy to forget how to appreciate them because of the pressure of what they feel. They keep back a little piece of their heart just if they're wounded in the future.

They can't permit themselves to fall deeply in love because they are terrified of all that love. After all, it could be a lot for them to manage.

Empaths are selfless people who are day-to-day bombarded with sensory info, so they typically feel like they carry a heavy load.

www.ingramcontent.com/pod-product-compliance
Lightning Source LLC
Chambersburg PA
CBHW071122030426
42336CB00013BA/2173